SUCCESS FOR ACTORS

PSYCHOLOGY FOR ACTORS SERIES

ALEXA ISPAS

WORD
BOTHY

CONTENTS

INTRODUCTION

Success is fleeting, they say. The feeling of success, even more so.

How many times have you reached a milestone in your acting career, only for the euphoric feeling of victory to dissipate before you even had the chance to acknowledge your achievement?

How long did it take for your old insecurities to reappear, while people were still congratulating you?

If this sounds familiar, you may find it reassuring to know there is nothing wrong with how briefly you were able to enjoy your new-found success.

For important evolutionary reasons, your feelings of elation are short-lived.

The so-called "happy chemicals" in your brain, which give you the energy and drive to work towards success, stop flowing as soon as you experience it.

As if that was not bad enough, these happy chemicals are replaced by cortisol, the "stress hormone."

Cortisol changes your brain chemistry in a way that makes you think, "There is a problem–watch out!" but does not give you any clear path to resolving this uncomfortable feeling.

From an evolutionary perspective, these post-success effects were beneficial for the survival of our species.

The fading positive feelings and rising sense of alarm gave our ancestors an incentive to reach even higher, instead of resting on their laurels and going hungry as a result.

However, as an actor living in our modern day world, this post-success chain of events can make it difficult to maintain and build upon your existing success.

If you are not aware of the changes in your brain chemistry, and how these changes affect your state of mind, you are likely to interpret the fading of positive feelings and rise in cortisol as a problem to be solved urgently, rather than a quirk of evolution.

This may lead you to engage in self-sabotaging behaviors that undo all your hard work, damaging your friendships and reputation.

The good news is that understanding how your mind works can help you skillfully navigate the complex thoughts and feelings that arise during the post-success phase.

Using psychological insights, *Success for Actors* will teach you how to approach the emotional rollercoaster of success with a healthy mindset.

The success we will explore in this book is not just the star-on-the-Hollywood-walk-of-fame kind.

We will also address the sense of accomplishment that comes with reaching small yet important milestones in your career, such as getting your first TV credit.

If you can learn not to sabotage yourself after experiencing these small yet significant milestones, you will be better equipped to handle big-time success.

Through reading this book, you will understand what is likely to happen in your mind at various stages of the post-success journey.

You will also learn how to make the most of

every bit of success you achieve, instead of veering into self-sabotage.

As a result, you will keep building on your existing success, reaching ever greater heights, instead of burning bridges and having to start over.

To prepare for success, you will learn simple yet powerful tools that will help you avoid self-sabotage and build on your existing success.

These tools, drawn largely from psychology, are presented in clear and jargon-free language, so you will be able to apply them straight away.

In the final chapter, we will discuss how to prevent self-sabotage after reaching various success milestones over the course of your acting career.

By the time you finish reading this book, you will be equipped for whatever level of success comes your way.

I have kept this book short, so you can read it in an afternoon and gain all the tools you need to thrive, even when the good feelings associated with success start to fade.

CHAPTER 1

SUCCESS: AN EMOTIONAL ROLLERCOASTER

SUCCESS AND SEROTONIN

To be successful is one of our most frequently expressed wishes as humans.

We want to be recognized for what we have accomplished, to be praised and applauded for the talents and skills we bring into the world.

As an actor, success is perhaps even more important than in other career paths.

The visibility inherent in this profession comes with a heavy dose of shame and self-doubt as a consequence of failure; a heavy price to pay for being unsuccessful.

Experiencing success as an actor is usually associated with being placed above others.

This is obvious given the many kinds of awards within the industry, but you can also see it at a more fundamental level, if you consider how casting works.

Good parts are rare to come by, and when they do, only one actor can get cast in a role.

If you are that person, you are likely to feel special, chosen, more talented, or in other ways better than everyone else who auditioned.

When you succeed as an actor, by getting cast in a great part, winning an award, or anything of that nature, your brain rewards you with serotonin.

This so-called "happy chemical" improves your mood and sense of well-being as a result of doing better than your peers.

The bigger the discrepancy between yourself and another actor—the more successful you are in relation to them—the more serotonin your brain releases.

Experiencing a sense of superiority in relation to your peers does not make you a bad person. It is part of being human, because of the way our brains have evolved.

The survival of our entire species depended on our ancestors striving to reach ever greater heights within their social hierarchy.

When they reached a new level, their brain rewarded them with a delightful serotonin boost that motivated them to reach even higher.

This quest to improve our status within our peer group weighs heavily on our minds to this day.

As an actor, it is essential to understand this powerful evolutionary urge.

SUCCESS AS AN EVOLUTIONARY STRATEGY

Living in groups–as our ancestors did–has led us to develop brains that continuously monitor our place within our social environment.

As soon as our ancestors' immediate needs were met, such as securing enough food, they turned their attention to advancing their place-ment in their social hierarchy. They craved success.

When competing with opponents they identi-fied as weaker, serotonin would start flowing in anticipation of victory.

Then, at the peak moment of victory, our ancestors would receive an even bigger serotonin boost.

This was nature's reward for achieving success,

and also a means of making our ancestors strive to reach even higher.

Those of our ancestors who fought to be higher ranked than their peers gained more access to food and other resources.

As a result, they lived longer and had more opportunities to pass on their genes.

Because of this evolutionary history, our brain has evolved to continuously monitor how we are doing in relation to our peers and to strive ever higher within our social circles.

The more we keep reaching, the higher our chances of re-experiencing the pleasurable sensations of success.

From this evolutionary perspective, your striving for success within the hyper-competitive acting industry is not just about a desire for recognition.

At a deeper level, it is a quest for survival.

THE ADDICTIVENESS OF SUCCESS

When you get a big boost in serotonin, everything feels right with the world.

At such moments, you have more energy and

self-confidence than usual, your immune system is at its strongest, and you generally feel amazing.

A sense of safety and well-being permeates your whole being.

Getting a big boost in serotonin–being success-ful–is an addictive feeling.

Once you experience this feeling you are bound to crave more, no matter how much success you have already achieved.

AN EVOLUTIONARY TWIST

With this exhilarating sense of your own power comes the expectation that the positive feelings associated with success will last.

Unfortunately, this is not the case. As soon as your brain releases its biggest reward at the height of your success, it stops releasing serotonin.

You are entering the post-success phase.

Why does your brain stop releasing serotonin at that moment?

Because from an evolutionary point of view, serotonin is no longer needed.

Nature has delivered its reward for all your hard work in reaching this new level; the only way to get more serotonin is to achieve something even more remarkable.

Simply repeating your previous achievement won't do.

For example, the first time you get cast in a film, you will get a big serotonin boost, which will give you a tremendous sense of accomplishment.

However, the second time you get cast in a film, your brain will not release as big a dose of serotonin.

To get as big a boost as the first time, you will need to reach an even higher level of success, such as winning an award for your work on the film.

This may seem cruel, because repeating a significant accomplishment, such as getting cast in a film, takes a lot of effort. It feels like the reward should be the same.

Yet when you think about this through the lens of evolution, it makes sense.

The reason you crave serotonin in the first place is to have an incentive to push yourself harder.

If you could get the same amount of serotonin every time for a particular accomplishment, you would not be motivated to reach higher.

Instead, you would be content with your

current level of achievement and stop striving for more.

What if our ancestors became content with what they had achieved, and stopped trying even harder?

We may be a lot happier, but we would still live in caves, or we may even have disappeared as a species because of some predator wiping us out.

The message from evolution is clear: no matter how high a level you reach, your competitive brain wants you to keep striving.

Ambition is coded into every aspect of your being. Nature wants you to reach higher, ever higher, and never stop craving more.

CONFUSION AND THE POST-SUCCESS PHASE

When actors experience the start of the post-success phase, they are usually unaware of this cruel evolutionary twist.

As such, they are utterly confused by the sudden change in their inner state when serotonin stops flowing.

"I should be happy right now–why am I not? What is wrong with me?"

For a feeling that is so universally desired, it is astounding how briefly we can enjoy our success.

Outwardly, you still look successful, but due to the changes in brain chemistry, you no longer *feel* successful—or you are starting to doubt whether you are successful enough.

The bigger the serotonin boost—the bigger the sense of accomplishment—the more debilitating the post-success phase feels.

In some cases, due to the visceral impact serotonin has on your sense of well-being, a big dip may even feel like a threat to your survival.

The better you understand what is going on with your brain chemistry, and why these exhilarating feelings don't last, the easier it is to cope with the fading of these positive feelings.

In addition, the less likely you are to misinterpret the fading of positive feelings as a problem.

In the next chapter, we will explore another big change in your brain chemistry that also happens during the post-success phase and that requires particular care not to misinterpret.

- When you experience success, your brain releases serotonin, a "happy chemical" that makes you feel superior to your peers.
- This boost in serotonin was instrumental in the evolution of our species. Our ancestors were motivated by serotonin to reach ever higher in the social hierarchy.
- When you get a large serotonin boost, everything feels right with the world; this is an addictive feeling.
- Once the peak moment of success passes, your brain stops releasing serotonin, because it is no longer needed from an evolutionary perspective.
- The only way to get another big serotonin boost is to achieve an even higher level of success.
- The more significant the success you experience, the bigger the serotonin boost, and the more painful it feels when the serotonin flow stops.

CHAPTER 2

A RISING SENSE OF THREAT

CORTISOL RISING

Your serotonin going down is not the only unpleasant brain chemistry change that happens during the post-success phase.

When your brain stops the flow of serotonin, it also starts releasing cortisol, the "stress hormone."

In contrast to serotonin's exhilarating effect, cortisol makes you feel anxious, giving you the impression that something is wrong.

Your immune system and mental health benefit whenever you experience an increase in serotonin, and suffer when your serotonin comes down and your cortisol rises.

It is as if your body is saying, "There is a problem–watch out!" and also, "Do something!"

Your cortisol rising generates an uncomfortable feeling in your body, putting you on alert without offering any clear path for resolution.

As a result of this sense of danger, you start worrying about everything that could go wrong, including losing your new-found success.

LOOKING OUT FOR THREATS

Other mammals who share these brain chemistry changes don't ask themselves why they no longer feel happy once they achieved a significant advancement in the social hierarchy.

When serotonin stops flowing and cortisol makes their body feel uncomfortable, they simply aim for an even more significant advancement.

Humans, on the other hand, usually respond to the post-success changes in their brain chemistry by looking for the cause of their unhappiness.

Our tendency to look for a cause is largely due to our prefrontal cortex, one of our main so-called "threat detectors."

This part of our brain developed late in our

evolution and is more complex in humans than in other species.

The prefrontal cortex helps, among other things, with logical reasoning and visualization, but it also has several other features worth mentioning.

Firstly, when the rise in cortisol signals that something might be wrong, your prefrontal cortex starts searching for potential threats.

Secondly, your prefrontal cortex does not exclusively rely on things you can see in front of you while conducting this search.

Instead, this highly sophisticated part of your brain gives you the ability to create abstractions, including threats, that feel real.

You can imagine something bad happening in the future, instead of having to wait for your senses to tell you that there is a danger.

This ability to imagine potential threats gave our ancestors an evolutionary advantage.

It allowed them to take preventative action against deadly threats and thereby keep themselves safe.

However, as a newly successful actor in today's world, this ability can terrify you into taking ill-advised actions that undo all your hard work.

A third feature of the prefrontal cortex is that

more of the input going to your eyes comes from your brain than from the outside world.

As a result, when looking for threats, your expectations influence what you see.

Is the director favoring another actor over you?

Are your fellow actors conspiring against you?

Are you in danger of getting fired?

If you expect to see a problem, this is what your eyes will see, as they are more heavily influenced by your prefrontal cortex than outside reality.

A FAULTY INTERPRETATION

If you start looking for threats, you will find them–whether they are real or not.

Your sophisticated prefrontal cortex can zoom in on the tiniest potential danger and–through the power of your imagination–make it seem like a huge problem.

When you find yourself under the influence of cortisol during the post-success phase, there is a chance that the threats you perceive are not as serious as your mind would have you believe.

More likely, your prefrontal cortex makes them seem more dangerous than they really are.

If you don't know how to rein in this tendency

to catastrophize and imagine horrible things happening, you can terrify yourself with your own thoughts.

In addition, the competitive nature of the acting industry is likely to make these threats appear even worse.

In the next chapter, we will explore how working as an actor within an overcrowded industry compounds the negative effects of these brain chemistry changes on your mental health.

KEY POINTS

- In addition to stopping the flow of serotonin during the post-success phase, your brain also releases cortisol, the "stress hormone."
- Cortisol leads to an uncomfortable feeling in your body and directs your attention to potential threats.
- It is easy to misinterpret this feeling as indicating that something is wrong. In fact, this is simply a feature of your brain's natural process during the post-success phase.

- This change in your brain chemistry puts you on alert, generating an uncomfortable feeling in your body.
- In an attempt to resolve this feeling, your prefrontal cortex starts looking for threats.
- Using its highly evolved features, it can create terror-inducing scenarios that exacerbate your sense of danger by mis-using your imagination.

CHAPTER 3

STOKING THE FIRE OF INSECURITY

.

COMPETITIVENESS WITHIN THE ACTING
INDUSTRY

Over the previous chapters, we explored two
changes in brain chemistry that happen when you
experience success.

These changes are rooted in our evolution and
lead to significant emotional turmoil.

The first change relates to serotonin, a so-called
"happy chemical" that your brain releases in anticipation of outdoing your peers while you are
striving for success.

As soon as you experience the peak moment of
success and get the big serotonin boost you were
craving, your brain stops releasing serotonin, as it is

no longer needed from an evolutionary perspective.

This sudden dip in serotonin leads to a desperate longing to recapture that amazing feeling of security and well-being.

The second change is an increase in cortisol, the "stress hormone," which creates anxiety and an uncomfortable feeling in your body.

Taken together, these changes in brain chemistry lead to confusion and a growing sense of threat.

Just as you have achieved everything you wanted, you start worrying.

Because of the way your prefrontal cortex works, if you look for threats, you will find them.

As more of the input going to your eyes comes from your brain than from the outside world, you see what you expect to see.

This chain of events, which happens to everyone who experiences success, regardless of their occupation, is made even worse by the competitive atmosphere within the acting industry.

From your earliest days as an actor, you have been competing with your peers for a small number of roles.

You are probably so used to having to fight for

every tiny opportunity that it has become second nature.

However, this constant state of alert also means your brain is extra vigilant when anticipating problems.

When your prefrontal cortex starts looking for threats within this competitive atmosphere, it is likely to find a myriad of dangers to bring to your attention.

ALLOWING FEAR TO INFLUENCE YOUR DECISIONS

Two fears are likely to stand out: the fear of being replaced by another actor and the fear of missing out on an amazing opportunity.

Within the competitive atmosphere of the acting industry, it is easy to think someone is always waiting to take your place.

This pre-existing sense of threat is likely to get worse once you have something valuable to lose.

If you have been a struggling actor for many years, your new-found success probably feels too good to be true.

Your prefrontal cortex may therefore take any possibility of getting fired and blow it out of proportion, presenting you with all sorts of horror-inducing scenarios.

The other fear, of letting a great opportunity pass you by, is caused by the fact that once you experience success, you are likely to find new doors opening for you.

As a result, you may have to make big decisions at dizzying speed, and not yet have the right people in place to advise you on which opportunities to take and which to turn down.

You may therefore take every opportunity that is on offer for fear of missing out.

These and other similar fears make you crave one thing above all else: a sense of security in your new position, the kind you briefly experienced at the peak moment of success.

To fulfill this need, you put all your energy into consolidating your new status within the acting industry.

THE "IF ONLY" FALLACY

In an attempt to gain a sense of safety, you are likely to fall into the "if only" fallacy.

"If only I reach such-and-such level of success, I can finally relax," you may tell yourself.

When you are under the influence of this fallacy, you believe that by working hard, you will be able to solidify your new status and recapture the sense of security associated with serotonin.

In the next chapter, we will explore workaholism—a natural consequence of this fallacy.

KEY POINTS

- The competitive nature of the acting industry compounds the sense of threat that arises during the post-success phase.
- You may fear being replaced by another actor and losing your new-found success, or missing out on a great opportunity.
- All such fears stem from a fundamental need for safety.
- You will likely strive to fulfill your need for safety by pushing yourself harder, hoping to solidify your new status.

CHAPTER 4

THE HAMSTER WHEEL OF SUCCESS

SEEKING A SENSE OF SAFETY

In the previous chapter, we discussed some of the fears that actors experience during the post-success phase.

In an attempt to alleviate these fears, one of the temptations during the post-success phase is to push yourself harder, chasing ever more success.

You believe that if only you could reach the next level up on the success ladder, you would recapture that feeling of inner security that serotonin provided.

As we will discuss in this chapter, because of the way your brain works, this cannot happen.

Instead, pursuing this illusory sense of peace

will only leave you more frustrated and put you at risk of burnout.

AN IMPOSSIBLE QUEST

As I mentioned in chapter 1, because of evolutionary reasons, your brain will only deliver a big serotonin boost the first time you accomplish something significant.

After that, to get another serotonin boost of the same magnitude, you will have to achieve something even more spectacular.

Unless you do, the previous type of accomplishment won't lead to the same feel-good result as before.

As an actor, this presents a significant problem.

If you seek to re-experience that initial state of bliss, you will soon come up against a deep sense of powerlessness.

Given how little control you have over your career, you cannot keep reaching greater heights within the industry whenever you feel down.

Even if things went amazingly well for a continuous stretch of time, expecting to keep yourself in a state of perpetual bliss will lead to disappointment sooner or later.

For example, you may get a big serotonin boost when you get cast in your first major production.

Then another big boost when you get cast as a lead.

And perhaps yet another boost if one of your projects becomes amazingly successful.

But where do you go from there? Does it take winning an Oscar or a Tony Award to finally feel content? And then what?

If you keep chasing success, you will always want more. This is how serotonin works.

As the sense of security you crave keeps edging further into the distance, you will feel increasingly frustrated and dissatisfied.

SUCCESS IS RELATIVE

Another reason your quest for a sense of security is bound to fail is that what counts as success is relative.

How much serotonin your brain releases depends not only on how well you are doing objectively, but also on where you focus your thoughts.

Reaching a new level in your career will expose you to actors who are doing better than you.

As you meet people who have achieved even

more and you start thinking how to ascend to their level, new horizons will appear before you.

Depending on how (in)secure you feel, that is not necessarily a good thing.

There will always be someone doing better than you.

As soon as you think of that person and the ways they are "superior," your serotonin goes down.

No matter how hard you work to become even more successful, your prefrontal cortex will keep directing your attention to all the ways you could be pushing yourself harder.

In a misguided attempt to gain a sense of peace, you may push yourself beyond your limits and slip into workaholism.

THE DANGERS OF WORKAHOLISM

Initially, workaholism may look like boundless energy.

You may start taking on more projects than you can handle and feel slightly overwhelmed.

Yet over time, workaholism is likely to become a much bigger problem.

Instead of allowing yourself time and space to

enjoy the fruits of your labor and recover your energy, you start chasing ever more success.

Although your work ethic may look admirable from the outside, you are working hard because of fear, rather than genuine enthusiasm.

By trying to re-experience that glowing feeling of success, you are likely to burn yourself out.

In the next chapter, we will explore how this frustrating chain of events can turn into self-sabotage.

KEY POINTS

- At the beginning of the post-success phase, you are likely to push yourself to recapture that sense of inner security that serotonin provided.
- Because of the way your brain works, this is an impossible quest.
- Your brain is not designed to deliver the same amount of serotonin twice for the same type of accomplishment. This means you cannot recapture those initial feelings of security unless you achieve something even more significant.

- Given how little control you have over your career as an actor, you will soon be faced with your own powerlessness.
- In addition, success is relative, and there is always someone doing better than you. Thinking of them stokes your insecurities.
- Chasing success will leave you frustrated and dissatisfied, as the sense of security you crave edges further into the distance.
- In trying to consolidate your new-found status within the acting industry, you will likely slip into workaholism.
- While your work ethic may look admirable from the outside, if you do not allow yourself time to relax and recharge, you are putting yourself at risk of burnout.

CHAPTER 5

SUCCESS AND SELF-SABOTAGE

ENGAGING IN SELF-SABOTAGE

In the previous chapter, we discussed how chasing success will leave you increasingly frustrated and dissatisfied.

No matter how hard you try, the sense of security you crave keeps edging further into the distance.

To numb your emotional pain, you start looking for anything that gives you relief from the effects of cortisol: alcohol, drugs, unhealthy food, and toxic people.

You may also engage in other self-sabotaging behaviors, such as being attention-seeking, controlling, or defensive.

In doing so, you are attempting to recapture the buzz and attention you crave, and that the peak moment of success briefly offered.

The problem is that using these unhealthy ways of numbing your emotional pain only provides temporary relief.

In addition, these types of behaviors are likely to burn bridges with those who contributed to your success, threatening to destroy all your hard work.

WHEN ATTENTION STARTS TO FADE

To add to this, your hard work will likely yield less impact the further you are from the peak moment of success.

Given the fast-paced nature of the acting industry, your time in the limelight will come to an end.

Although you will encounter other successful times in the future, this particular cycle is drawing to a close.

As this starts happening, you are likely to experience a sense of fading of attention as everyone's focus shifts elsewhere.

Even if you know this is bound to happen, it is a painful experience.

Our brain is equipped with so-called "social pain circuits."

These circuits developed when we depended on others for taking care of us as babies, and we carry these circuits into our adult years.

When attention starts to fade and you see your impact diminishing, a sense of abandonment activates these social pain circuits.

The ancient parts of your brain trigger the fear that if you do not get attention from the people you depend on, such as your agent or your director, you will die.

In such circumstances, it is easy to lash out at members of your team, blaming them for not doing enough for you.

If you give into this temptation, you put yourself at risk of burning bridges with some of the most important people in your life and driving yourself deeper into isolation.

BECOMING ISOLATED

To make matters worse, your friends and members of your team may not realize what is going on for you, underneath the surface.

Unless they have gone through a similar situation, they may not know about the brain chemistry changes you are going through, and how challenging these changes can be.

As far as they can see, you have everything you ever wanted.

They may even express envy at how far you have come, increasing your feelings of isolation.

If you do not take the time to explain to them how you feel and how the post-success changes are affecting you, they may not understand the reasons for your unhappiness.

As a result, the brain chemistry changes that happen during the post-success phase put you at risk of isolating yourself from your friends, family, and other members of your support network.

These are the very people who gave you the emotional sustenance to achieve success, and whose support you need to be grounded and happy in your everyday life.

A NOTICEABLE DECLINE IN MENTAL HEALTH

All too often, we hear of actors who experience a decline in their mental health following a brief period of success, despite having enviable work and lifestyle opportunities.

A significant gap emerges between how your life looks from the outside–successful, financially secure, in high demand–and how you feel on the inside.

You can have everything anyone could ever wish for, but if you have poor mental health, you will not be able to enjoy the fruits of your labor.

Because of self-sabotage, your success may be gone before you realize what is happening.

However, none of these consequences are inevitable.

In the next chapter, we will start exploring a range of tools you can use to avoid self-sabotage and make the most of every moment of success you experience.

KEY POINTS

- As soon as the peak moment of success passes, everyone's attention shifts elsewhere.
- A sense of abandonment activates your "social pain circuits" and makes you feel like your survival is under threat.
- To numb the emotional pain, you may be tempted to use alcohol, drugs, and

other unhealthy means, but these only provide temporary relief.

- You may also attempt to recapture the attention you crave by blaming members of your team for your diminishing success and by being controlling or defensive.
- This behavior will likely burn bridges with those who contributed to your success and threatens to destroy all your hard work.
- Your friends may not understand what is going on for you, accentuating your feeling of isolation.
- Over time, your mental health is likely to go into decline unless you find a way to break this cycle.

CHAPTER 6

PREVENTING SELF-SABOTAGE

PREPARING FOR SUCCESS

Success can happen quickly within the acting industry, and it can be big.

One day you may be a struggling actor, having spent years knocking on doors and not getting anywhere, while battling financial difficulties and dejection.

Then you could get cast in a dream role and become hot property, your whole life changing overnight.

We all know actors whose lives were completely transformed, for better or worse, as soon as their big moment came.

Although initially exhilarating, this emotional rollercoaster can also constitute a challenge.

Because of the rapid changes in your brain chemistry and life circumstances, this kind of upheaval puts you at risk of developing mental health problems.

Some actors are able to come out of this period of turmoil relatively unharmed, but this is rare, especially for those who encounter a significant level of success.

Perhaps you are lucky to have a supportive family, or someone who knows how to help you navigate the tumultuous times that come with success.

But even if you are among the lucky few with this level of support, it is best to put preventative measures in place to keep yourself safe.

The better prepared you are for success to happen, the less the post-success phase will desta-bilize you.

AWARENESS IS POWER

The negative consequences of entering the post-success phase are not inevitable.

However, the traps are difficult to avoid, and

your mind–influenced by the changes in your brain chemistry–can trick you into self-sabotage.

It takes wisdom and good mental health habits to navigate this confusing territory.

The sequence we have explored over the past few chapters–feeling elated when experiencing success, then confused once the happy feelings fade away, then anxious and worried about potential threats–is a consequence of our evolution as a species.

In other words, this pattern lives deep within your psyche, and not something you can change.

The good news is that once you become aware of this sequence, you can recognize it when it happens, instead of allowing yourself to get swept away by the emotional rollercoaster.

With awareness comes the opportunity to reassure yourself and find your way around the complicated feelings that will likely arise.

As a result, you can spare yourself the agony of falling prey to your unfounded worries and slipping into self-sabotage.

DEVELOPING A SET OF TOOLS

There are many tools that can help you cope with the post-success phase.

You can redress the sudden brain chemistry shifts you will experience during the post-success phase by learning how to boost your happy chemicals, as we will explore in chapter 7.

By influencing your brain chemistry intentionally, you will no longer be at its mercy, nor will you feel as bereft when the good feelings associated with serotonin fade away.

You can also learn to boost your self-confidence and keep any threat-focused thoughts in check, as we will discuss in chapters 8 and 9.

These tools will help you combat self-sabotage by converting your sophisticated prefrontal cortex from an enemy into a powerful ally.

And finally, you can implement a set of preventative measures so that when you encounter success, you can deal with the post-success phase in the best way possible.

This includes getting into healthy habits, such as celebrating milestones and taking time off, instead of pushing yourself beyond your limits, as we will explore in chapter 10.

These preventative measures may seem to slow you down, but they actually speed you up in the long run.

The goal in learning these tools is to give yourself an anchor that will counteract the destabilizing effect of rapid changes in your brain chemistry.

Having these healthy habits in place will make it easier to take any changes in your circumstances—for better or worse—in your stride.

In doing so, you will avoid slipping into self-sabotage and undoing all your hard work.

Over the next few chapters, you will learn how to prepare for the post-success phase, starting with tools that help you rebalance your brain chemistry.

KEY POINTS

- The potentially sudden nature of success in the acting industry exacerbates the impact of brain chemistry changes on your state of mind.
- Understanding how your mind works can help you navigate the complex thoughts and feelings that experiencing success brings up.

- You can also learn how to maintain your balance when going through the difficult post-success times.
- This means you can keep building on your existing success instead of sabotaging your hard work and having to start over.

CHAPTER 7

BOOST YOUR HAPPY CHEMICALS

CRAVING SEROTONIN

As you know by now, improving your mood does not mean recapturing the feeling of success at its peak; that is impossible.

However, you can improve your mood by lowering your serotonin cravings.

To do so, you can learn to boost one or more of your other three happy chemicals: your endorphins, dopamine, and oxytocin.

Reducing your serotonin cravings is similar to improving your relationship with food.

If you have already experimented with this, you may have learned not to eat the high-fat, high-sugar foods you crave, but feed your body with something healthier that helps reduce your cravings.

You can apply this same principle to reducing your serotonin cravings.

Endorphins, dopamine, and oxytocin, all improve your mood and lower your cortisol.

Even a small boost in one of them can reduce your serotonin cravings and allow your brain chemistry a chance to rebalance.

Boosting your happy chemicals will also help you avoid the temptation to indulge in other unhealthy ways of soothing yourself, such as binging on junk food or using alcohol and drugs to numb the emotional pain.

HOW TO BOOST YOUR HAPPY CHEMICALS

Boost your endorphins

Endorphins are part of your body's pain relief mechanisms. This includes the low-level pain that comes as a result of physical effort.

When you exercise and your body releases endorphins, you do not feel this low-level pain reverberating through your body.

Instead, you are flooded with a pleasurable

sensation that acts like an analgesic. This pleasurable sensation is caused by endorphins.

Not only does this boost in endorphins make your body feel great, but it also reduces your cortisol.

This is why physical exercise helps so many people clear their minds.

The easiest way to boost your endorphins is to do some physical exercise.

This exercise should be strenuous enough to reach a threshold of low-level pain, as this is what triggers your body into releasing the endorphins.

One great thing about endorphins is that you can boost them whenever you like, regardless of what is happening in your environment.

Go for a run, or do some other strenuous physical exercise, and you will lower your cortisol within minutes.

You will soon find yourself in a better mood than before, with fewer threat-focused thoughts clouding your mind and a sense of calm permeating your whole being.

Boost your dopamine

Your brain releases dopamine when you set your eyes on a "reward," such as a goal or something new that comes to your attention.

Just like releasing endorphins, dopamine is easy to boost, as it does not depend on other people.

The quickest way to boost your dopamine is to set an easily achievable goal.

This goal can be anything you like: a household chore, such as cleaning your living space, or a creative goal, such as working on a painting.

I would advise you to look for a goal that is unrelated to acting–such as searching for auditions in your area–because that might remind you of your serotonin blues.

Try to distract yourself from acting for a while with something different.

Another easy way to stimulate dopamine is to learn something new.

You could learn a new skill, such as playing the piano, or read a book that engages your mind and helps you gain perspective.

Boost your oxytocin

Oxytocin is your so-called "cuddle hormone."

You get an oxytocin boost whenever you have a sense of belonging within a community.

A word of warning: boosting your oxytocin may be more difficult to achieve than the other two happy chemicals, because it depends on how others respond to you.

In addition, bonding with others takes time, so this is not a quick fix.

On the other hand, oxytocin may be the most effective way to reduce your serotonin cravings.

When you experience a sense of belonging with certain people, you feel safe, and therefore have less need to prove yourself to the world.

As such, despite the difficulty and the time it may take to encourage your brain to release oxytocin, it is worth the effort.

Where do you feel you belong?

Do you already have a group of people around you who give you that sense of belonging and support?

If not, where would be a good place to find such people?

If you need a quick oxytocin boost and don't

have the time for bonding, there are other ways to encourage your brain to release oxytocin.

For example, a massage or the sensation of soft textures on your skin also stimulates oxytocin, as does anything else that makes your body feel comfortable.

A SKILL YOU CAN PRACTICE

Which happy chemical you choose to boost depends on what works best for you and what is feasible within your particular circumstances.

You may already have a way of boosting one or more of these happy chemicals, in which case you'll know that those strategies definitely help you when going through a difficult time.

If you are unsure what works best for you, try experimenting with each of these happy chemicals and see which one makes the biggest difference in lifting your mood.

You can also try boosting all these three happy chemicals at the same time, to compound their positive effects.

For example, you could arrange to go on a hike with a few of your friends.

The hike would give you a goal to reach

(dopamine), while also being physically straining (endorphins), and providing you with a sense of belonging (oxytocin).

Be aware that all happy chemicals fade away after an initial boost and are replaced by cortisol.

Do not expect to keep yourself in a state of perpetual bliss.

However, knowing how to boost your happy chemicals puts you in control of your mood.

This will make the dip in these natural mood-boosters less worrying.

In the next chapter, you will learn another set of tools you can use to combat the effects of cortisol on your state of mind during the post-success phase.

With the help of these tools, you will be able to reduce any feelings of insecurity you might have by boosting your self-confidence.

KEY POINTS

- You can reduce your serotonin cravings by boosting one or more of your other three happy chemicals: endorphins, dopamine, and oxytocin.

- To boost your endorphins, do some strenuous physical exercise.
- Boost your dopamine by setting an easily achievable goal and reaching it within a short time frame, such as a day or a week.
- You can boost your oxytocin by bonding with others. Alternatively, you could get a massage or use soft textures to give yourself that comfortable feeling in your body.
- Boosting your happy chemicals is a skill you can practice and use to shift your mood and avoid slipping into self-sabotage.

CHAPTER 8

BOOST YOUR SELF-CONFIDENCE

SELF-CONFIDENCE AS AN ANTIDOTE

Insecurity is at the root of self-sabotaging behavior during the post-success phase.

The more insecure you feel, the more this is likely to influence your perception, making it easy to slip into self-sabotage.

As such, one of the most effective ways to avoid this behavior is to work on your self-confidence.

When you feel confident, you are less at risk of allowing any changes in your brain chemistry to poison your thoughts.

Instead, you will have a sense of inner strength that will help you skillfully navigate your emotional ups and downs.

In this chapter, you will learn three simple yet powerful tools to boost your self-confidence when needed.

HOW TO BOOST YOUR SELF-CONFIDENCE

Your unique selling points

During the post-success phase, your brain will constantly attempt to trick you into comparing yourself to other actors.

When you fall into this trap, you make yourself insecure, which puts you at risk of self-sabotage.

One of the most important aspects of self-confidence is knowing who you are–what makes you unique.

The "unique selling points" tool can have a profound impact on your self-confidence throughout the whole course of your acting career.

To use this tool, ask yourself a few important questions:

- What do you bring to the table as an actor?
- How would a director who enjoys working with you describe you to a colleague?

- What kinds of stories can you tell through your physicality?

These questions may sound basic, but it is amazing how many actors have never spent the time to ask themselves what they have to offer.

As a result of this lack of self-knowledge, they keep themselves in a constant state of insecurity that influences their perceptions.

By regularly reminding yourself of your unique selling points, you will be less worried about your competition and avoid self-sabotaging behavior.

The pride smoothie

This second tool is especially good for your self-confidence day-to-day.

At the end of every day, take a few minutes to write in your journal three things you did that you are proud of; this is your pride smoothie.

The three things do not have to be acting-related. They can be anything you feel proud of, such as doing yoga, responding well to a setback, or fulfilling a promise to yourself.

This tool requires some discipline and consistency, but it is easy to use and its impact is cumulative.

Without conscious effort, your brain will not pay attention to the things you do well.

By using this tool every day, you are training your brain, particularly your prefrontal cortex, to pay attention to the things you do well and feel proud of.

With practice, your brain will more readily notice these things and your self-confidence will grow.

The writing aspect is important, as it allows you to keep track of things you are proud of over time.

By providing yourself with this much-needed acknowledgment, you will need less serotonin.

As a result, any praise from others will feel like a bonus rather than a necessity, and you will find it easier to bond with your fellow actors.

Your greatest hits

Make a list of your "greatest hits"–moments in your life when you felt successful and accomplished.

List as many such moments as you can remember, even small moments of success that make you feel good about yourself.

You can acknowledge times when you have been generous to others, or clever at coming up with solutions to a problem.

Include moments when you realized you had improved as an actor, as well as moments that have made you more rounded as a human being.

This list is a valuable resource in growing your self-confidence and banishing insecurity.

Put this list somewhere you can easily access and read it whenever you need a self-confidence boost.

Make sure you read the individual items slowly, remembering all the sensory details of the moments you have listed.

As you experience more success over time, update your list.

FIND STABILITY WITHIN YOURSELF

Practicing these self-confidence tools will help you feel more secure, which will make it easier to navigate the stormy post-success phase.

Even if you experience success on a large scale

and your outer life changes, you will not lose your sense of self.

If you find these tools useful and would like to delve deeper into this topic, I suggest you read my book *Self-Confidence for Actors*.

In the next chapter, we will explore a range of tools you can use to challenge any threat-focused thoughts that might arise during the post-success phase.

KEY POINTS

- Another way to avoid self-sabotaging behavior is to increase your self-confidence using simple yet effective tools.
- The "unique selling points" tool will help you identify what you–and only you–can bring to the table as an actor. The more you acknowledge what makes you unique, the less you will worry about your competition.
- The "pride smoothie" will direct your attention to the things you did during your day that you feel proud of and help you keep track of these over time.

- Your "greatest hits" will remind you of all the amazing things you have already accomplished throughout your life.
- Using these self-confidence tools will diminish your insecurity and help you retain a strong sense of self during the post-success phase, making it easier to avoid self-sabotage.

CHAPTER 9

TAKE CHARGE OF YOUR THOUGHTS

THREAT-FOCUSED THOUGHTS AND THE POST-SUCCESS PHASE

One of the most challenging aspects of entering the post-success phase is the sense of danger you are likely to experience.

This sense of danger takes hold of your thoughts and focuses your attention on threats to your new-found success.

When you find yourself in this situation, you must remember that you are under the influence of cortisol.

Because of cortisol, you are likely to see threats everywhere and be tempted to take ill-advised action in a misguided attempt to protect yourself.

"There's a problem, watch out!" says the cortisol-influenced voice in your head, making your body uncomfortable and prompting you to take action to protect yourself.

The problem is that the actions you may undertake during this post-success phase will likely lead to self-sabotage and undermine your previous efforts.

To ease your discomfort and avoid slipping into self-sabotage, you must re-direct your attention away from potential dangers.

In this chapter, you will find a set of tools that will help you take control of your thoughts and steer them in a positive direction.

If you have already read my book *Resilience for Actors*, you will know that these tools were originally developed by Martin Seligman and colleagues as a way to overcome pessimistic thoughts when encountering a setback.

However, you can also use these tools during the post-success phase to counteract the sense of danger that arises from the influence of cortisol on your state of mind.

TOOLS TO SHIFT YOUR THREAT-FOCUSED THOUGHTS

Look for contrary evidence

The most obvious way to take control of your threat-focused thoughts is to question the evidence on which they are based.

When you are under the influence of cortisol, your thoughts are likely to be distorted by a sense of impending danger.

As a result, once you start looking for evidence, you are unlikely to find any.

For example, let's say you just got cast in a small yet memorable part in one of the most anticipated films of the decade.

Once the peak moment of success has passed and you are entering the post-success phase, you may start experiencing "imposter syndrome."

What if this is too good to be true?

What if another actor would have been a better choice, and it is only a matter of time before the casting team realizes it?

What if you will be fired in a public and humiliating way on your first day on set?

If you notice these kinds of thoughts, you need

to intervene and prevent cortisol from wreaking havoc on your extraordinary accomplishment.

Ask yourself, is there any evidence to support your thoughts?

Once you ask yourself this simple question, you will likely find no actual evidence.

These thoughts arise because of cortisol triggering your prefrontal cortex into imagining all the things that could go wrong; the dangers you imagine are not real.

To go even further, you can look for contrary pieces of evidence.

Write a list of all the qualities you bring to this role and remind yourself of the unique selling points you identified in the previous chapter.

These qualities are unique to you; no other actor has your specific mix of energies.

By taking the time to reflect on your unique qualities, you will be able to reassure yourself and avoid self-sabotage.

This process, lasting no more than a few minutes, will make it easier to dismiss any threat-focused thoughts from your mind.

Reframe your thoughts

If you suspect there is some evidence that justifies your sense of danger, yet the likelihood of something going wrong is low, another way to avoid self-sabotage is to use "reframing."

Redirect your attention towards a more optimistic interpretation of the situation.

For example, let's say you have started work on your best acting job to date.

Once you are in the post-success phase, you start thinking, "The director spends far less time with me than with the other actors. It is clear they are biased against me."

The way to reframe this is to look for a positive interpretation of the situation.

As you try this method, you may find some of the alternative explanations too optimistic.

For example, you may think, "The director is spending less time with me than the other actors because my choices align with their vision. They are therefore letting me get on with what I am doing."

If this sounds too good to be true, remember that threat-focused thinking consists of the reverse.

This includes latching on to the most threatening alternative–such as the director planning on firing you–not because of evidence, but because it resonates with the sense of danger generated by cortisol.

De-catastrophize your thoughts

Another way threat-focused thoughts may show up for you is through a tendency to catastrophize–"Making a mountain out of a molehill."

When you catastrophize, you take something negative that has a basis in reality and you turn it into the worst of all possible scenarios.

Let's say you recently started work on a film.

A few days into filming, under the influence of cortisol, you find yourself thinking, "The director doesn't like me and is looking to fire me. Maybe I should quit, to avoid humiliation."

When you notice yourself catastrophizing, ask yourself, "What is the evidence for this way of looking at the situation?"

You are probably going to find a few bits of evidence that support your threat-focused thoughts.

Maybe a particular scene did not go as well as you had hoped and the director seemed disappointed with the result.

Ask yourself, "Is there an alternative way of viewing this situation?"

You can probably think of several instances where the director appreciated your work.

However, these are not likely to be as memorable until you put in the effort to remind yourself.

This is because, as humans, our perceptions are distorted by the so-called "negativity bias:" we have a tendency to pay disproportionate attention to the negative aspects of our lives.

As a result of this bias, we have a better memory for things that go wrong than for things that go well.

However, when you shift your attention to the things that went well in the past, you can counteract the effects of this bias on your memory.

Once you realize the situation is not as bleak as you initially thought, it becomes easier to come up with a more positive evaluation.

For example, your new interpretation could be, "The director likes my work on this project overall, but was not keen on my latest choices."

This alternative is more specific and gives a clear indication of what needs sorting out.

As such, it allows you to be proactive in a way that is empowering to you and others.

For example, you could ask to speak with the director, to understand what they disliked about your choices and find a solution moving forward.

By critically examining your threat-focused thoughts instead of behaving impulsively, you can avoid turning your fears into self-fulfilling prophecies.

Instead, you are giving yourself the opportunity to take action that is helpful to everyone.

Question the usefulness of your thoughts

Sometimes, the consequences of having a particular thought are worth considering.

For example, a thought such as, "Everybody is out to get me," may cause more trouble than it's worth.

Even if you suspect others are envious of your success and would love to take your place, what good will it do to dwell on that possibility?

Instead of asking, "Is this true?" ask yourself, "Is this useful?"

If the answer is no, then redirect your focus away from this way of thinking.

Distract yourself

This tool is a short-term strategy that you can use in situations when you notice your threat-focused thoughts, but do not have the time to apply any of the other tools at that moment.

For example, while starting the first day of a new dream job, you may be gripped by a sudden fear that you are not the right person for this part and that it would be better to resign.

This is a classic case of imposter syndrome caused by the influence of cortisol.

If you find yourself in this situation, distract yourself, do what you need to do, and then use the other tools when you have time to spend on the matter.

One way to distract yourself is to undertake a physical action to bring your attention back to your body.

For example, you can slam the palms of your hands against a hard surface or snap a rubber band against your wrist.

By switching your attention to something physical, you are interrupting your threat-focused self-talk.

This gives you space to direct your attention elsewhere and quieten your mind.

Another way to distract yourself is to pick an object in your environment and focus on it for a few moments.

You could also engage with that object in a sensory way, by handling and smelling it.

A third way to distract yourself is to schedule your self-talk for later.

In this way, focusing on it in the present moment no longer makes sense and you can get on with what you need to do.

HOW TO APPLY THESE TOOLS

The tools in this chapter take a while to learn and practice.

However, dismantling your threat-focused thoughts is worth the effort, to avoid undoing all your hard work.

Which tool is the most effective depends on the situation you find yourself in and the specific thoughts running through your mind.

Initially, I advise you to go through all these tools any time you identify a threat-focused thought, as each can help you in a different way.

You will soon get a sense of how to use these

tools in practice and the benefits each of them brings.

Over time, you will probably develop preferences for some tools over others.

For example, if your threat-focused thoughts have a catastrophizing tendency, you may find the de-catastrophizing tool particularly effective.

In the next chapter, we will explore a range of simple yet effective tools you can use to develop a good sense of grounding within yourself.

KEY POINTS

- When you notice you are being influenced by cortisol during the post-success phase, you need to take charge of your thoughts to avoid slipping into self-sabotage.
- You can examine the evidence supporting your thoughts, or reframe them into a less threatening alternative.
- You can also challenge your threat-focused thoughts on the basis that they are too extreme, or that they are unhelpful and disempowering.

- You also have the option of distracting yourself from your threat-focused thoughts by focusing your attention elsewhere.

CHAPTER 10

DAY-TO-DAY PREVENTATIVE MEASURES

PREPARE YOURSELF FOR SUCCESS

As you no doubt realize by now, dealing with the post-success phase can be difficult.

Navigating this period gracefully requires preparation.

The more tools you have to keep yourself grounded, the better you will cope with the emotional rollercoaster that accompanies success.

In this chapter, you will find a set of simple yet effective measures you can take during your day-to-day life to prepare.

You may already be doing some of these things. If so, you are on the right track and have a solid foundation on which to build.

These measures will help you maintain a good sense of balance no matter what circumstances you find yourself in.

FINDING BALANCE AS AN ACTOR

Pace yourself

Give yourself lots of rest and self-care instead of relentlessly pushing forward with your goals.

Don't wait until you "make it" to finally take a break.

As you know by now, no matter how hard you push yourself, and for how long, you will always feel that you need more success to be completely secure.

This is especially true within the competitive atmosphere of the acting industry.

Taking breaks and time off may look like you are slowing down, but in fact, such preventative measures will make your efforts sustainable long-term.

Self-care will allow you to build energy reserves you can deploy when needed.

By taking good care of your mental health before anything else, you are ensuring that you can maintain the success you have already achieved.

Instead of sabotaging yourself and undoing all your hard work, you will be able to build upon the solid foundation that comes with having good mental health habits.

Celebrate your success

Although, as we have established, it is not possible for the happy feelings that accompany the moment of success to last, it is possible to prolong their effect.

To do so, take the time to acknowledge and celebrate your success.

Don't immediately jump into the next thing. Take as much enjoyment out of that short moment of happiness as you can.

The easiest way to do this is to get into the habit of celebrating every career milestone you reach.

By celebrating every milestone, you give yourself the opportunity to fully acknowledge your success before the joyful feeling fades away.

It is easy to forget, when your brain chemistry changes during the post-success phase, how amazing your achievement is and how far you have come.

At such times, it is tempting to focus on the threats that could ruin your success and what you could do to reach even higher, instead of acknowledging what you have accomplished.

By setting the intention to celebrate every milestone, you are taking preventative measures against this all-too-common scenario.

Every time you celebrate your success, you are insulating yourself against the effects of cortisol during the post-success phase.

In addition, you are making memories that you can recall in the future, whenever you need a self-confidence boost.

Make time for non-acting pursuits

One way to ensure you are not veering into self-sabotage is to ask yourself, what else are you doing that brings you joy, besides acting?

It may seem counter-intuitive to spend some of your limited spare time on non-acting pursuits. Shouldn't you devote yourself to your craft?

The trouble is, if acting is the only thing in your life that brings you satisfaction, you will be more likely to fall into self-sabotage during the post-success phase.

It is easy to lose perspective when you see dangers around every corner and have nothing else to focus on.

To prevent this from happening, devote some of your time and energy to non-acting pursuits that are meaningful to you.

Do volunteer work, find a fulfilling hobby, spend time with your loved ones.

The more enjoyment you can derive from your non-acting life, the less you will suffer from the changes in your brain chemistry during the post-success phase.

When you feel down because of something that relates to your acting career, you can use the other aspects of your life to find joy.

This will make it easier to replenish your happy chemicals, instead of letting cortisol take over and tempting you into self-sabotage.

If, while reading this, you realize you have little in your life apart from acting, then this is the time to introduce one or more non-acting pursuits.

That way, when you find yourself in the post-success phase, you will not try to achieve the impossible and recapture the elation you experienced at the peak of your success.

Instead, you will have other ways to feed your

soul while you wait for the next success cycle to begin.

Recognize success cycles

Many believe that there is a linear progression to success: you go from being unsuccessful to being successful and living happily ever after.

However, as the years pass and you go through the many ups and downs of your acting career, you will likely realize that a long career is made up of a variety of success cycles.

There will be times in your life when you will be on an upwards trajectory, reaching higher and higher levels of success.

And then you will reach the post-success phase and start seeing others overtaking you as your star begins to wane.

The good news is that if you avoid self-sabotage and burning bridges as this happens, you put yourself in a great position for the start of the next success cycle.

As an actor, you are not in control of the timing of that new beginning, but you can enjoy the rest of your life and trust that another cycle will soon begin.

By being kind and gentle even when a particular success cycle is coming to a close, you are building a growing support network around you who will accompany you through all the twists and turns your career will take.

Learn to recognize the wisdom in the cyclical nature of success; do not resist the post-success phase.

By allowing yourself to experience the difficult moments of that cycle, instead of numbing the emotional pain, you will gain compassion for your fellow actors as they travel through their own dark places.

During moments of crisis, you will know how to help those who need your unconditional support.

Your wisdom will be a shining beacon of strength in the darkness.

STAYING DOWN-TO-EARTH

"Don't let success go to your head," people often say when you finally get the recognition you deserve.

This sounds like good advice, but how do you do it?

The tools in this chapter, although simple, provide a practical solution.

Implementing these tools in your everyday life will allow you to keep yourself grounded when success comes.

The more level-headed you can remain when you experience success, the less destabilizing the changes in your brain chemistry will be.

As a result, it will be easier to get through the post-success phase without resorting to self-sabotage.

Develop a good level of self-knowledge before success comes, so you know what works when your career suddenly takes off.

Many things are not within your control as an actor.

Yet how you respond to external changes is something you can control; this includes the way you respond to success.

The better prepared you are, the less destabilizing it will feel to experience the post-success phase.

As a result, you will benefit from your success and use it as a stepping stone for the next stage in your career.

In the final chapter, we will explore specific

post-success situations you may encounter over the course of your acting career.

KEY POINTS

- To deal with the post-success phase well, you need to prepare by learning how to keep yourself grounded.
- Staying grounded at all times will make it easier to cope with the changes in brain chemistry resulting from experiencing success.
- Pace yourself. Don't race towards the finish line. The positive feelings you expect will not last and you will soon be chasing the next goal. Instead, build time into your days, weeks, and months, to relax and recharge.
- Celebrate your successes. This will help you experience the happy feelings associated with success for a longer period. You will also make beautiful memories that will give you strength in years to come.
- Make time for non-acting pursuits. This will allow you to find balance and

a sense of perspective, regardless of the twists and turns your acting career might take.

- Prepare for the next success cycle. Instead of trying to recapture the peak moment of success, start preparing for making the most of your next opportunity.

CHAPTER 11

SUCCESS AND THE ACTING LIFE

EXPERIENCING SUCCESS AS AN ACTOR

Your expectations of success influence the way you will experience the post-success phase.

If you expect the blissful feelings associated with success to last, you will be anxious and confused when those brief moments of elation fade away.

Suddenly deprived of serotonin and flooded by cortisol, you are likely to see threats everywhere.

As a result, the descent into self-sabotage is likely to come swiftly.

By contrast, if you know the happiness associated with success is fleeting, you will make the most of those brief moments and then calmly acknowledge their passing.

You will also be aware of the influence of cortisol on your state of mind, and know how to navigate the complicated thoughts and feelings that arise without jumping into ill-advised action.

The post-success phase may still be a somewhat difficult transition period, but you will have more choice in how you respond to the changes in your mood and sense of well-being.

In this chapter, we will explore a series of challenging post-success situations that you can make easier by applying everything you have learned in this book.

TROUBLESHOOTING SUCCESS

What follows is not a complete list of all the things that could happen in the future associated with experiencing success.

It is simply a way to start considering various moments in your acting career when you might experience the post-success phase.

By learning to recognize those moments when they arise, you will be able to navigate those potentially challenging times with ease and grace.

Reaching a career milestone

Success means different things to different people, depending on where you are in your acting career.

Reaching a career milestone–the first time you get cast, your first speaking part in a feature film, your first significant stage role–are all moments of success when you may experience all the elements of the post-success phase.

Be careful at such times, and use all the knowledge and tools you have learned in this book to make the post-success phase as easy as possible.

By practicing going through the post-success phase with relatively small wins, you are building the confidence and skills to deal with more significant levels of success.

Getting cast in a dream role

Getting cast in a dream role is one of the most likely ways you will encounter success in your acting career.

The experience of being chosen for a dream role from among many other actors, after several rounds of auditions and callbacks, is bound to lead to a huge serotonin boost.

As a result, once the serotonin stops flowing and the post-success phase sets in, the changes in brain chemistry are likely to feel especially difficult to handle.

Deprived of serotonin and under the influence of cortisol, you may suddenly be plagued by "imposter syndrome" and start imagining all the ways your beautiful dream could turn into a nightmare.

Because of the way the prefrontal cortex works, if you start looking for threats, you will find them.

To avoid falling into this trap, ignore all the catastrophizing thoughts going through your mind.

Do not allow imaginary threats to turn into self-fulfilling prophecies.

Instead, challenge your threat-focused thoughts using the tools you learned in chapter 9.

In addition, rebalance your happy chemicals as you learned in chapter 7, and boost your self-confidence using the tools in chapter 8.

In particular, go through your "greatest hits" to remind yourself how amazing you are and how much you have already accomplished.

Once you feel calmer, direct your attention to how you will celebrate this achievement.

By rewarding yourself, you are placing your

focus on positive things and making beautiful memories for the future.

Proving your superiority over other actors

Another potentially dangerous scenario that often happens during the post-success phase is attempting to boost your serotonin by making your fellow actors feel inferior.

You know that actor who has an even better story than yours, or who has achieved even bigger success and keeps telling everyone about it?

When you are under the influence of cortisol during the post-success phase, it is tempting to behave in this way to get a serotonin boost, not realizing you are making it harder to bond with your fellow actors.

The feeling of superiority that serotonin gives you is short-lived, but the loneliness you will experience when you behave in this way will continue, unless you change your attitude.

By becoming aware of your serotonin cravings, you will find it easier to avoid slipping into this type of behavior and put your energy into bonding with others instead.

When interacting with your fellow actors, focus on connecting in a meaningful way.

Doing so will boost your oxytocin and reduce your serotonin cravings.

When you focus on creating genuine connections, your fellow actors will enjoy spending time with you, which will give you a sense of belonging.

This kind of mood boost is longer lasting than serotonin and makes your heart feel good.

Even your career will benefit–who wants to work with someone who is arrogant and domineering?

We all seek people who are kind and make us feel good about ourselves; by being that person, you will attract all sorts of positive things into your life.

Many acting projects are short-lived, but if you are in this industry long-term, you will meet your fellow actors again.

How do you want them to remember you?

If you tend to slip into competitive behavior when feeling insecure, you can change this pattern.

Keep focusing on connection instead of competition, and over time, you will grow out of this self-sabotaging tendency.

Fighting for resources

Being competitive with your fellow actors can also show up in a more tangible way: noticing any resources that other actors have access to and wanting these resources for yourself.

Your prefrontal cortex, always on the lookout for threats, may bring uncomfortable questions to your attention.

Is that other actor getting more pay than me?

Are they getting more publicity?

Why is their name ahead of mine on the bill?

Motivated by the need for serotonin, your brain continuously scans your environment to determine where you are placed in the social hierarchy.

If you find someone who is getting access to a desirable resource–increased publicity, better representation, more money–your brain releases cortisol, leading to an uncomfortable feeling in your body.

In nature, this cortisol release has two functions.

If an animal sees itself as weaker than another animal, the cortisol release makes them hold back, thus avoiding conflict with the more powerful animal.

On the other hand, if an animal feels stronger than the other animal, the discomfort generated by cortisol will motivate them to challenge that other animal to a fight.

Although it makes sense from an evolutionary perspective, this competitive tendency can tempt you into sabotaging your working relationships with members of your team.

You may risk falling out with your agent, your manager, your publicist, or whoever else you blame for the fact that another actor is getting better treatment.

If you find yourself in this situation, use the tools in chapter 7 to rebalance your brain chemistry, the ones in chapter 8 to boost your self-confidence, and those in chapter 9 to challenge your threat-focused thoughts.

Once you find yourself in a better mood and are less influenced by cortisol, it is time to make an honest assessment of the situation.

It could be that the problem is simply in your mind. If so, once you use the tools you learned in this book, you will realize that all things considered, the treatment you are receiving is fair.

On the other hand, not every problem you see during the post-success phase is a matter of out-of-balance brain chemistry and distorted perception.

Some of the problems you identify are real, and in that case, they cannot be solved psychologically.

There may be times during the post-success phase when you are right to question the treatment you are receiving.

If you have a persistent feeling that you are not well represented, or that you are receiving worse treatment than you deserve, you may have to take action.

Do not let your ability to find a sense of inner calm become a barrier to initiating much-needed change.

Feeling overlooked

Feeling overlooked by a specific person you depend on is particularly common in an actor's life, especially during the post-success phase.

You may feel overlooked when your agent pays more attention to a recent client than to you, or by a director who treats your performance with indifference while fawning over another actor's choices.

Whenever you feel overlooked, you must figure out whether your assessment reflects an actual problem, or whether your insecurities are distorting your perceptions.

Try to see the situation from the other person's point of view.

Ask yourself, from that vantage point, if you are being treated unfairly.

Use the tools you learned in chapter 9 to challenge any threat-focused thoughts you may have, to prevent such thoughts from distorting your perception of reality.

As mentioned in chapter 5, your brain is equipped with so-called "social pain circuits," which originally developed when you were a baby and depended on others to take care of your needs.

As an adult, when feeling overlooked by the people you depend on, these neural circuits give you the sense that your survival is in danger.

This is not a conscious thought, but it activates the release of cortisol.

As such, when these neural circuits come into play during the post-success phase, they provide a powerful motivator to "do something."

The resulting impulsive actions often end up burning bridges with members of your team.

If you find yourself in a situation where you

feel overlooked by a person you depend on, refrain from taking impulsive action.

Ask yourself whether your assessment of the situation might be influenced by these old brain circuits that motivate you to seek attention at all cost.

On the other hand, having given yourself the space to make an honest assessment of this kind, you may determine that you are indeed being overlooked by this person.

In this case, you must figure out what to do to change the situation in a way that does not damage your working relationship.

For example, if you are being overlooked by your agent, maybe you need to refresh your agent's memory of you.

What might be a good way to do that?

Simple gestures, such as a thoughtful card thanking them for all their help over the years, may work wonders.

Whatever you do, make sure not to veer into self-sabotage.

Avoid burning bridges with the people who have helped you on your path.

They may just need gentle reminders, from

time to time, that you still need their help and attention.

When attention shifts elsewhere

One of the most painful moments during the post-success phase is when your star begins to wane.

Perhaps you became hot property for a while, but all too soon, the opportunities dry up and you don't know how to get back in the game.

The realization that progress has stalled and your career is going backwards rather than forwards is a difficult yet common experience among actors.

This sense of backwards motion is often compounded when you see previously less successful actors gaining traction and leaving you behind.

The more you achieve within the industry, the more difficult it will be to see previously obscure actors getting ahead.

The problem is that, as an actor, many important factors that impact your career are not within your control.

As such, focusing on how others are doing will

likely make you feel helpless and put your mental health at risk.

In these situations, you are in danger of veering into self-sabotage.

This may include reaching for alcohol and drugs to numb the emotional pain, or burning bridges with members of your team.

To avoid self-sabotage, shift your focus to areas of your life that are within your control.

In addition, allow yourself to acknowledge how far you have come.

You have accomplished extraordinary things and it is time to celebrate your wins.

By celebrating your achievements, you are putting yourself in a positive state of mind and replenishing your energy.

This will give you a small serotonin boost, perhaps less than you would like, but enough to keep you away from self-sabotage.

In addition, use all the tools outlined in chapter 10 to start preparing for the start of the next success cycle.

By taking small steps every day to keep yourself grounded and in good spirits, you will be in an excellent place for when the next major opportunity comes your way.

INCREASING YOUR AWARENESS OF SEROTONIN

As you consider the scenarios we explored in this chapter, and perhaps others that are relevant to you, I encourage you to direct your attention to your brain chemistry's influence on your state of mind.

Learn to recognize the signs of serotonin boosts and cravings while your life is relatively stable.

Now that you have started thinking about serotonin and its connection to success, you will start noticing when you get small serotonin boosts here and there.

You will also become more aware of your thoughts once the pleasurable feeling associated with those changes fades away.

Over time, you will find it easier to recognize how your serotonin cravings, and the associated rise in cortisol, influence your thoughts and feelings on a day-to-day basis.

You will also have the opportunity to practice shifting your thoughts and feelings by using the tools you have learned throughout this book.

Over time, you will find it easier to cope with

these brain chemistry fluctuations and know what to do to maintain your balance.

By preparing in this way, you will be ready to take on the type of upheaval that accompanies a significant accomplishment.

By developing these skills, you are turning your sensitivity into a strength and building a solid foundation for your acting career.

CONCLUSION

Handling success well requires preparation.

If you are at a stage in your career where you are still striving for success, this is the perfect time to start preparing for when your big moment comes.

It takes a lot of skill and conscious effort to find your way through the post-success phase without damaging your mental health.

As part of that, you will need to learn to turn your brain into an ally instead of letting it draw you into self-sabotage.

One of the most important take-away messages throughout this book is about the effect of serotonin on your state of mind.

As you learn to become more aware of the

changes in your brain chemistry in the context of your acting career, you will also start applying this understanding to other areas of your life.

This new awareness will not just make your acting career better—it will improve your whole life.

In this way, your acting career will become a path to self-growth, with all its twists and turns.

Getting a handle on your serotonin, and your brain chemistry in general, takes practice.

You often won't notice your threat-focused thoughts until you will find yourself obsessing over them, by which time you will be swimming in cortisol.

This is a natural thing to happen while changing your thought habits, so do not beat yourself up over it.

Acknowledge your thoughts and use the tools in this book to get yourself out of your self-sabotaging patterns.

The fact that you have read this book to the end and are taking proactive measures to prepare for success is already a step in the right direction.

Remember that you are unique, so tailor everything you have learned to your own needs.

Use this book as a starting point for developing your own process.

Please consider passing on this knowledge to any actor friends going through a difficult time because of how they handle the post-success phase.

They will benefit and be happier for it, and you will become a beacon of strength and empowerment in their lives.

I wish you all the best with your acting career.

I would like to ask you for a small favor.

Reviews are the best way to spread the word about this book. If you have found this book helpful, it would mean a lot to me if you could leave a review.

Even if you write only a sentence or two, it will help. Thank you!

A USEFUL RESOURCE

If you want to improve your chances of success as an actor, psychology can help.

Psychology Tools for Actors teaches you ten simple yet powerful psychology tools to take your acting career to the next level.

Download for free when you sign up for the *Psychology for Actors* newsletter at:

www.psychologyforactors.com/newsletter

ABOUT THE AUTHOR

Alexa Ispas holds a PhD in psychology from the University of Edinburgh.

The books in her *Psychology for Actors Series* provide actors with proven psychology techniques to thrive and build a successful career.

If you'd like to stay in touch with Alexa and learn more psychological tools that are directly relevant to actors, please sign up for the *Psychology for Actors* newsletter. You will receive a short free book when you sign up.

You can sign up for the newsletter and receive your free book at:

www.psychologyforactors.com/newsletter

Memorization for Actors

Self-Confidence for Actors

Resilience for Actors

Motivation for Actors

Excellence for Actors

Success for Actors

For more information, please visit:

www.psychologyforactors.com

Printed in Great Britain
by Amazon

22959774R00065